Seeing you from a distance made me Cuckoo…

By Khadijah Johnson

Published by Eternal Impartation
For more information regarding publishing, editing, proofreading and book cover design please contact us.

3536 University Blvd. N, Ste 181
Jacksonville, FL 32277
(904)566-0514
www.eternalimpartation.org
eternalimpartation@gmail.com

All rights reserved under Copyright Law. Contents and/or cover may not be reproduced in whole or in part in any form without the express written consent of the Publisher.

Edited and proofread by V F Johnson, Steward Unlimited
Cover Design by Farris Long, Longevity Graphics & Printing

Copyright © 2011 Khadijah Johnson
All rights reserved.
ISBN: 0615510736
ISBN-13: 978-0615510736

TABLE OF CONTENTS

Endorsement

Dedication

Acknowledgments

Foreword

Table of Contents

Chapter 1
    The First Time I Saw You   7
    The Decision   12
    The Dream   17
    The Next Few Weeks   24
    The Word is Out   27
    Pursuing   36

Chapter 2
    Frustrated, Fed-up, I Entertain the Counterfeit   39

Being Led	46
Sow Seed in the Right Season And Soil	54

Chapter 3
Power of Persuasion	58

Chapter 4
Back to the Dream	74

Chapter 5
The Revelation	90
Feeling Unworthy or Of Little to No Value	97
The Soul of a Man	101
God's View of Us	104

Chapter 6
My Life's Journey	106
What Does It Mean To Be Christ Like	111
Who I Am	115
Let's Pray	120

ENDORSEMENT

Today living in a society that wants instant gratification, it is refreshing to see the inward working of Holy Spirit in the life of this author. In this book she puts forth a challenge to live by God's word and demonstrates it in her sharing truthfulness of the inward parts to help to be real with ourselves. I am encouraged even more with transparency in life with the Lord. In genuineness with ourselves, we can then walk in freedom in our relationship with Him being naked and not ashamed.

       V F Johnson, Steward Unlimited

DEDICATION

NOTICE: PLEASE READ!!!!

The dedication of this book is for you the reader. I wrote this book especially for you. Praying that as you read this book joy, laughter, liberation and transformation will come into your life and those you may connect with in days, weeks, or years to come. As you began reading; **Seeing You From a Distance…** don't just read it just to say I have read something. Read it with expression and expectation to get what you need out of it.

I encourage you to read this book more than once. Because I guarantee you that what you may have missed the first time will definitely empower and influence you the next time.

ACKNOWLEDGEMENTS

I am so grateful to have a wonderful family. Who would have known that my mom would give birth to a bunch of creative, prophetic, business minded women? To my sisters thank you for your creativity, prayers, prophetic words, and your support. I love you sooo much.

To my mom thanks for being my example in the earth that at the age of sixty something you are still able to fulfill destiny and vision. I love you!

God has blessed me with three wonderful children who never stop loving me. I love you more than words express and I thank you for making my life joyful. You are mommy's babies.

To my prophetic ladies I am grateful that we had a chance to connect, support and push each other into purpose. Much love to ya!

To Jesus my Lord, my Savior, and my Redeemer I honor You, I glorify You, I give You all the praises; my soul makes it boast in You. Hallelujah, glory to God, You are worthy Lord. There is none like You in the heavens nor in the earth I will bless Your Holy name. I will forever praise You! Gloryyyy!

FOREWORD

This book is not a typical book. I encourage each reader to open himself or herself up to the transparent life of my beloved friend. This book is what I consider what the scripture declares that God will give you beauty for ashes. This is a portion of Khadijah's life and how she reveals herself to help others to come into deliverance, self worth and value knowing that you don't have to walk in anyone else's shadow to get to your destiny.

Khadijah's journey reminds me of the duck who through different situations and circumstances in life looked like the ugly duckling and now has evolved into this beautiful swan.

My advice for those reading this book is to be open to the truth and not narrow minded and judgmental.

To Khadijah my words to you … but this one thing I do, forgetting those things which are behind and reaching forth unto those things which are before, 14 I press toward the mark for the prize of the high calling of God in Christ Jesus (Philippians 3:13-14 KJV).

Conquer and go forth,
Apostle Stanley L. Roundtree

Chapter 1: The First Time I Saw You

The First Time I Saw You!!!

It's the summer of 2010, I just finished a prayer call, and before I could close my eyes for the night, I told the Lord that I am going to settle my emotions. That's when I had my first dream about you since last year of 2009 and in that dream I saw you standing a short distance from me as tall as you are with a white button-down shirt and what I believe was a pair of dark denim blue jeans. There you stood at least six feet two inches tall, bald-headed with those pretty, brown eyes.

You turned and looked at me saying, "Khadijah you are my bride, my wife" and I said, "Ok" as we went further down the hallway. You stopped again and said, "Khadijah, you are my bride, my wife." My response

Chapter 1: The First Time I Saw You

as still the same, "Ok." When I woke up I said, "Wow God it is what it is and I choose to believe You."

Not sure, of the exact month it had to be the beginning of fall or maybe the end of August of 2005 when we met. The ministry I attended hired a new youth pastor; all the youth workers had to come together to meet our new youth pastor and to go over new ideas and strategies to help with the progression of our youth. We sat in those cushioned red chairs chatting with each other patiently waiting for this person to arrive.

Finally walking towards the front of the room from behind us is a tall guy who seemed to be about three hundred pounds plus wearing a green shirt, blue jeans and green and white sneakers. As he begins to introduce

Chapter 1: The First Time I Saw You

himself a small voice within me said, "This is your husband." Responding back to the voice I said, "Nah, this must be my flesh talking because he is not even my type." Tuning my ear back to what he was saying he speaks in a loud clear voice and said, "I am not here to be anyone's husband. I'm your brother in Christ and you are my sisters in Christ." I was like ok God that confirmed it for me; he is not the one. As time goes on, we learn to adjust to the changes that were being made in the youth department.

Even though our youth pastor didn't live in the city or state we lived, he did his best to fly in every other week trying to maintain balance and have a good relationship with the teenagers and youth workers. He was able to impart in us different ways to minister to the youth as we imparted

Chapter 1: The First Time I Saw You

back into him through prayer and intercession. It seemed as if the youth ministry really was moving forward or going along smoothly, but as time goes on division starts to break out amongst the workers.

Pastor Black was deemed the star in our place of fellowship. Our old youth pastor was excellent in what he did, but he was also very traditional in his approach towards the teenagers. Now here comes a man who is prophetic, comical, and whose strategy to reach the teenagers was non-traditional. He decided that we should have our own teenage club that would minister through drama and skits. He also suggested that we start a step team. What a great idea! That was out of the box for us; it was something we have never seen nor done before.

Chapter 1: The First Time I Saw You

Several months had passed before jealousy and competition begin to manifest among the workers, which turned into a hot mess. We had those who wanted to become the next best youth worker or the pastor's close friend. People started talking about people; it was just crazy and it started to get out of hand. With all that was going on, I battled for weeks whether or not to stay or to leave the youth ministry.

Chapter 1: The Decision

The Decision!!!

    I concluded that I was no longer going to be a part of the youth ministry. Looking at the calendar to see when Pastor Black next scheduled weekend was to come to Jacksonville, I began to rehearse what I was going to say. It was the Sunday of his return to Jacksonville and I remember getting dressed for church wearing my pin striped navy blue pants, with a baby blue turtleneck and my baby blue, snake skin, printed heels I felt ready and confident, except I wasn't going to my home church that morning.

    After I got out of church, I called up my friend Nita and asked her did our youth pastor come in town today. She responded, "Yes." I told her I needed to meet with him and she said, "He's going to be at my house

Chapter 1: The Decision

today." What a perfect opportunity I thought to myself. She came over to my house to pick me up and she questions me about what it is that I wanted to talk to him about. "Why," I asked. Her response was he thinks that you want to marry him. In shock I replied, "What on earth gave him that idea, or why would he think that?" Now I'm really nervous because I don't know what to expect.

    Remember early in the chapter I said a voice within me said that he was my husband. We walk in the front door of her home with me still dressed as sharp as a tack as we head to the living room. He sits there with his arms stretched across the back of their leather couch with this big smile on his face, as if he is waiting to see what it is I have to say. By this time, I am a nervous wreck. He's thinking one

Chapter 1: The Decision

thing and I'm truly there for another reason. Taking my seat next to him on the couch he blurts out, "So what is it that you want to talk to me about. Before I could respond with an answer, he responds, "Is it that you want to be my wife and have my son" looking at him in total amazement I responded, "No." He said it again, "So you are telling me that you don't want to be my wife and have my son." Thinking to myself, did he not hear me the first time when I said no? Whether he was serious or not for the rest of the night he made suggestions about me becoming his wife and even referring to my children as his own.

    The night grew long and he departed, while his armor bearer stayed behind. As the conversation stirs up about what just happened, his armor bearer tells us that he is still in a

Chapter 1: The Decision

relationship with another woman. I was HOT and I showed him just how much via e-mail. The e-mail went something like this: Pastor Black when I sat and looked at all that was going on I truly had to go to God. So here it is...

    1. *I believe you need to get your flesh under control.*
    2. *What is your motive for trying to pursue me? See one thing I don't like is games; I've done that and I am just a little too old to play. I then told him that I've already been married and I've had sex so those things don't impress me. Please don't make me lose the respect that I have for you; my children especially my daughter looks up to you as a man of God.*

    I went on telling him what he always told us that his heart would let

Chapter 1: The Decision

him know when he has found the right person. Reminding him that the Bible said that out of the heart flow the issues of life and is very wicked too (Proverbs 4:23, Jeremiah 17:9, Luke 6:45). My question to Pastor Black was what's in your heart. I then prayed for him and ended my e-mail.

Chapter 1: The Dream

The Dream!!!

After being approached by several different males who proclaimed that the Lord told them that I was their wife, I had enough and decided to cry out to the Lord asking Him to show me who He has as a real husband for me. In 2002, my marriage of seven years had now ended. A single mother with three children ages seven, six, and two transitioning from two incomes to one was very difficult. I couldn't afford to stay in the apartment anymore so I had to give it up. My children and I moved into a friend's house which was a four-bedroom with two baths, but the thing about that was she already had two children and a husband. Therefore, we all had to stay in one room with two twin beds. (PJ if you ever read this I want to say thank you and I am so

Chapter 1: The Dream

grateful.) My children went from AB honor roll to Cs and Ds it was a difficult time all the way around financially, physically, and mentally for all of us. This experience is what drove me to question the Lord about whom my husband was because I didn't want to make the same mistake as before.

Let's take a break right here. I hear the Lord ministering to someone right now saying that it is not over for you. Whatever or whomever He has promised you it is surely going to happen. His promises for your life are yes and amen (II Corinthians 1:20). You have to believe that no matter what it looks like, that's not truly what it is. That's not the ending He has for you. You are going to make it and you can make it just put your trust in Him not man. I had put my trust in other things

Chapter 1: The Dream

therefore I got other things, but when I put my trust in God I got God things. Hallelujah! (It's time for a praise break.) Father I thank You for the person that is reading this right now. Bless my brother or my sister for putting their trust in You Now in Jesus name. Amen.

After praying to Daddy, the true and living God I cried myself to sleep. That night I fell asleep laying on my right side on the couch. I remember while lying there, I saw in my dream a house that I was in which looked similar to my mom's house at the time. The house had cream or beige looking tile on the floor in the living room, a fireplace, and a brownish, green colored sofa. In the middle of the floor were four or five wooden-back white cushioned dining room chairs that were gathered in a half circle.

Chapter 1: The Dream

The season or timing seemed to be Thanksgiving where there was a lot of family at the house. Sitting in the chairs were my mom and my three sisters, my brothers, and uncles were sitting on the sofa. The chair that I sat in stood out from the other chairs; that's when I saw this man get down on his knees and propose to me asking me to be his wife which at the time I still didn't see his face. While still asleep, I felt myself turn over on my left side and when I did, that's when I saw his face. He was bald with a full beard and those pretty brown eyes piercing at me asking me to take his hand in marriage and be his wife.

I woke up the next morning astonished by what I just saw and who the person was so I immediately jumped in the shower, and started contending with God. Daddy I said

Chapter 1: The Dream

this couldn't be; he is not even my type. For one he is extremely overweight and I don't do heavy people. Then I said well Lord, if it's Your will then ok, but in the next minute I'm feeling that it couldn't be true. After I got out of the shower, I picked up my cell phone calling up my friend Nita in disbelief of what I just saw in this dream. I said, "Girl I just dreamt that someone proposed to me." She then said the exact name of the person I saw whose face was our youth minister, Pastor Black. She then told me that she had a similar dream to mine.

Getting ready for church on this particular Sunday I didn't go to my home church the place where I fellowshipped, I went to visit a ministry across town. I remembered it so clearly as I came in the door and sat

Chapter 1: The Dream

on the third row while he was ministering. The Lord interrupted the service having a prophetic word spoken by the speaker saying, "I don't know who this is for, but you have been contending with God about whom your husband is and God said it is him, but it's in His timing." I sat there looking around at everyone else as if he wasn't talking to me. In a way, I wanted to hear that and then again, I didn't.

Let me tell you a little about the man the Lord showed me. First, he is an only child and a virgin he has no children. I know someone is saying girl what's wrong with that. He travels the nations preaching the gospel, has his own record label with two cds out at this time. He's a comedian appearing on television, producing and writing movies and he wants a son.

Chapter 1: The Dream

Whereas I am divorced, a single parent struggling to make ends meet and at the moment I don't want any more children. Lord how could this be?

Chapter 1: The Next Few Weeks

The Next Few Weeks!!!

Over the next few weeks it seemed that I was having dream after dream about this man and our wedding. On the first night, I saw us at the altar in all white. The second night I saw the details of my dress, which the top half was a halter-top style full of beads and the bottom was the new bunchy style that's out now. The third day I saw my four-karat diamond pear or rectangle shaped ring. Speaking to my best friend Nita over the telephone, I started telling her about the dreams saying, "Who dreams like this?" This has to be my flesh or maybe I thought about him subconsciously and that made me dream of him. She just laughed at me and said, "This just may be from God." Then the Lord started showing me

Chapter 1: The Next Few Weeks

details about his life and his ministry so now I am really tripping.

Believing this is whom God really showed me, I started to pursue after my dream, my destiny. He would send out a monthly message, which would be words of encouragement from his life experiences or through a prophetic word given by the Holy Spirit via e-mail. This was the main source of contact for me besides when I saw him.

I began to intercede not really knowing that what the Lord was truly revealing to me was actually, what he was going through in his life at that time. Every prayer that I sent out he would respond by mentioning something said in my praying for him in his monthly message. That told me he had gotten all of the prayers I had

Chapter 1: The Next Few Weeks

sent to him which some how gave me hope.

Chapter 1: The Word is Out

The Word is Out!!!

It's sometime in 2006 and the word is out about the e-mail I sent and about the dream I had of our youth pastor being my husband. I remember one particular day driving down Normandy Blvd in Jacksonville, Florida. I received a phone call from someone who shared with me that our Bishop's wife read the e-mail that I had sent to him and wanted to meet with me. I was terrified! I was surprised and wanted to know how she knew about this e-mail I sent out to him. Little did I know that the e-mail address I sent message to, certain people had access to it and she was one of the many that was able to access this message. Even though we never got the chance to meet (thank God hallelujah), the rumor spread that it was because of this e-mail I sent that

Chapter 1: The Word is Out

he decided to leave his position as youth pastor at our church. Still believing that he is part of my destiny as my husband and the father of my children I continued to pursue.

In April of 2006, he was doing this big production play in Atlanta, Georgia. I was not going to go so I prayed and asked Daddy again what I should do. If He wants me to go, then He is going to have to show me. There again I had a dream; in this dream I saw myself praying for some people and a phone number (404) _ _ _ 8179. I didn't know what exactly this meant so I started looking up what each number meant. Like the number four biblically means creation or earth, eight means new beginnings, one means unity, seven means completion and nine means fullness of

Chapter 1: The Word is Out

development. So I was trying to figure out how I can apply this to my life.

    When I got to work that next day I was telling my co-worker that I had a dream about a phone number and she said go and look the area code up in the phone book. One of Atlanta's area codes is 404 and this is what helped me in my decision to go.

    Traveling to Atlanta wasn't that easy; I had to travel with people who didn't like me because of the e-mail and the fact that I dreamt he was my husband. Tension was definitely in the air, but I pressed on. The morning of our departure I was told by some of those who were traveling with us that I was driving to slow and maybe I should just turn around and go back home. I told them I am not going back home, but for them to give me the

Chapter 1: The Word is Out

directions and I will get there when I get there. Their attitudes showed me right there that they really didn't want me to come.

As we continued down the highway I started to pray to God and said God I know that you would have me to go on this trip and because my car can not go as fast as their cars allow them to slow down. Guess what happened, they slowed down. Prayer makes things happen. We arrive at the hotel and I go to the counter like everyone else thinking that I was going to split the room cost with the ladies, but that didn't happen they told me I had to get my own room. I was like okay I see what's going on. I got my room showered and chilled for a moment before it was time to leave for the show. All of a sudden, the phone in my room starts ringing. I pick up

Chapter 1: The Word is Out

the phone and on the other end I hear Khadijah can one of us come and use your shower because it is too many of us in our room that need to shower before the show. I said to myself see that is what they get for trying to be nasty. However, being the person that I am I said of course with a smile.

We still get to the show extremely late. By the time we got to the show, they were ending the first half. We had to sit further in the back until intermission and then we could move to our original seats towards the front. That night I wore an all white skirt and jacket set with a light blue camisole under the jacket and some baby blue heels. Before the second half of the play began, we were able to move closer to our original seats four rows from the stage and I'm sitting in the third seat from the end. The lights

Chapter 1: The Word is Out

now dimmed down and he comes out from back stage wearing an all white suit.

What a coincidence that we are the only two in all white and the second half of his show dealt with how he wants to be married and he started singing songs from one of his albums. I became nervous and excited as if this was some kind of sign or clue. This sign convinced me even the more that the vision I saw was right; also the decision to pursue what I thought was destiny seemed certain.

By the end of the show, he starts giving God glory and honor. The Spirit of the Lord begins to move in him and amongst the people, so he begins to pray and prophesy to the people. He asked us to join him in prayer and we did. We were all

Chapter 1: The Word is Out

outside praying for people. This was the part of my dream where I had seen myself praying. After we finish praying for the people, we go to the after party and wait for his arrival.

All the people from Jacksonville were at one table. Little did I know that two of the women who were standing in front of me had the same thought as me that this was their husband too? It's funny now but back then I didn't think it was so funny. I don't know if they had a dream or if they believed the Lord told them that he was their husband, but we all were there to engage in what and who we believed was our destiny.

As the night comes to an end and he is just ignoring all of us we began proceeding to walk out of the door, when he grabs my hand walking next

Chapter 1: The Word is Out

to me he said, "How did you like the show and thank you for coming?" At that moment, I felt that there was a little bit of hope because out of the three of us who were there and had the same thought I was the only one he chose to have small talk with that night.

While we drive off and I am still on cloud nine, reality starts to kick in. Two other women actually believe along with me that this is their husband. All types of questions were running through my mind. Thinking to myself why would these women think that he is their husband too. What on earth has he told these women? Is he playing both of them or do they just assume that he is their husband? Doubt begins to set in and I'm thinking there is no way that this man can be

Chapter 1: The Word is Out

my husband because too many women feel the same way.

    I continue to struggle with believing that he is truly the one that God showed me in my dream. As time continued, I began to ask God for confirmation such as let someone bring up a conversation about him and this happened. Let him send out a message today so he did. Everything I asked of the Lord to help me believe he was the one. He did it. I felt like Gideon in Judges. God if You said this then let this happen; if this is you then let this happen. To me it still wasn't looking like a completed puzzle. Somehow, I felt that the pieces didn't fit and were not coming together. I continued looking at who I was and who he was and the fact that he wants a son and I have three children and not certain if I want another child.

Chapter 1: Pursuing

Pursuing!!!

Pursue means to find or employ measures to obtain or accomplish; to go in pursuit. When the Lord gave me a glimpse of my destiny, I started to pursue what I believed was purposed for my children and me. Sometimes when we are able to see a glimpse of our destiny we begin to pursue it without inquiring about the timing of the Father or we begin to work at our destiny through our emotions never reaping a true harvest.

As I shared this part of my fate or future with different ones, I allowed them along with myself to send me on an emotional roller coaster. I received comments, as God is not going to show a woman who her husband is before he shows him. Then I heard a

Chapter 1: Pursuing

man that finds a wife… (Proverbs 18:22) A woman doesn't find a man, a man finds a woman. Listening to all of these comments I simply said, "Why wouldn't the Lord show me who he is? It would keep me from making the same mistakes as before."

    It is very important that when getting that glimpse of destiny we seek the face of God concerning His timing. Ask Daddy to order your steps according to the word of God concerning how to take part in bringing your destiny to pass. There is a religious spirit that's saying we shouldn't question God, why not? Those in the Bible questioned Him all the time. Ask Him questions. Inquire of Him to find out what He is showing you about your destiny or is the picture bigger than what you are seeing.

Chapter 1: Pursuing

Everyone should know this one to keep immature people out of your business. If they are not able to take your vision into prayer with you and seek the face of God concerning it, keep it quiet! When we don't pursue our destiny in the right timing or if we do it through our emotions we become frustrated and upset. We start to get distracted thinking that it will never come to pass and we tend to get off track, by getting out of the will of the Father. This causes us to miss seeing the fruit of what we are pursuing.

Chapter 2: Frustrated, Fed-up, I Entertain the Counterfeit

Frustrated, Fed-up, I Entertain the Counterfeit!!!

It's 2007 and I am just about convinced that the dream I had was a type or shadow of who my husband really is. Around May or June of 2007, my green hatchback Daewoo had just kicked the bucket. Listening to the mechanic who told me not to put any more money into fixing this car, I had to go buy a new car. One Sunday after church a friend takes me to different car dealerships to shop for cars. Without having any success we call it a day and decide to head out the next weekend. She remembers that a friend of hers once dated a guy who was a general manager of a car dealership, so we decide to go there. When we arrive at the car dealership, I get out of the car and walk around the lot looking at the different vehicles and

Chapter 2: Frustrated, Fed-up, I Entertain the Counterfeit

their prices, knowing that I did not want to purchase another used car.

While I look at cars, she goes inside and gets the general manager. I glance up at the door of the dealership just as he is walking out towards me; all I see is this tall guy who is over six feet tall with a full beard and a bald head. Approaching me he sticks out his hand and said, "Hi my name is Lamar and anything you want on this lot you can have." I'm thinking he's very confident. Not seeing anything that really catches my eye, I tell him let me continue to check around. He politely gives me his card and said, "You'll be back." After going to several different car lots with no success I told my friend I better go back to the place were God has given me favor. I called Lamar and got his voice mail, so I left him a message

Chapter 2: Frustrated, Fed-up, I Entertain the Counterfeit

saying that I would be back to the dealership the next day to purchase a car. I arrive at the dealership around ten o'clock the next morning and he wasn't there.

So, I left and came back around twelve o'clock noon. Walking into the dealership wearing a pair of Capri pants with some type of heels I sit in this chair next to him as he pecks on the computer. He looks at me with this big smile on his face and starts to comment on my legs and how fine I was. Smiling I tell him thank you and asked him if he could please tell me if I qualify for a vehicle and what type. He tells one of the car salespersons the Vehicle Identification Number (VIN) to one of the cars on the lot giving him instructions to pull it around front.

Chapter 2: Frustrated, Fed-up, I Entertain the Counterfeit

Waiting to see what type of vehicle he's bringing, Lamar finds out that I am not married through the application process and then he starts making suggestions to another co-worker about why he is not married and that I could be his wife, to let me know that he wasn't married either. When the vehicle arrives he said take this home for two or three days and if you like it, then we will make the deal if not let me know and we will see what else we could do. Taking the car that was a 2007 Pt Cruiser home, my children and I loved it so we decided this would be the car. Returning to the car dealership two or three days later we finish up the paper work and he hands me the keys as I give him a thank you card which said I pray that the Lord will bless you just as much as He has allowed you to bless us. Then I got in my new vehicle and drove away.

Chapter 2: Frustrated, Fed-up, I Entertain the Counterfeit

Over the next couple of weeks, Lamar starts to call and text me. I didn't respond because my mindset at the time was partially hung up on the dream I had and the other part was I didn't want to play with his emotions, so I ignored him. He was very persistent! I remember getting a text that said something like hey how are you and I responded back by calling his phone. He was so excited that it just blew me away; it was as if he couldn't wait to hear my voice or for me to respond to him. We talk only for a few moments because he was in a meeting in Detroit, but I remember getting off the phone thinking that was different. His excitement was something I had never experienced. Laughing aloud and thinking this joker must be crazy I continued thinking about Pastor Black. Even though I was frustrated because I didn't see the

Chapter 2: Frustrated, Fed-up, I Entertain the Counterfeit

manifestation of the dream, somewhere in me I wanted to believe what I saw could still be true.

    A month has passed and it is time for me to go and get my car detailed; as the car is being cleaned, I go inside the dealership out of the heat. I take a seat in one of the chairs at this round table and out comes Lamar; he sits at the table with me and we start up a conversation. Once we shared with each other, we found we had some things in common. We both were divorced and had custody of our children. He is a believer in Jesus Christ and I am a believer in Jesus Christ. Leaving impressed I thought I would try this after all he is the first person I saw that came extremely close to the dream I had in 2005.

Chapter 2: Frustrated, Fed-up, I Entertain the Counterfeit

We continue to get to know each other by going out for lunch and talking on the phone. I remember one day I was at work and I just felt inspired to send him a cookie bouquet to his job. By the time I got home from work I received a phone call and on the other end was Lamar crying saying, "What is it that you're trying to do to me?" He goes on to explain how he never received anything like this before. He said that no one sends him anything and he is always the one that gives out to others. I didn't know it was that serious. I was just doing something that I felt led by the Holy Spirit to do and it blessed his life.

Chapter 2: Being Led

Being Led!!!

When we yield to the leading of the Holy Spirit, we are able to bless others without even trying. We as people don't always know what each other is going through, but the Holy Spirit will make it known to us without us even asking Him what that person needs. That is what happened to me I didn't know this would affect him the way it did. Nevertheless, God knew just what he needed on that day and at that particular time. Because Daddy loves us so much He will do that for us. So when you feel the unction of the Holy Spirit leading you to do something for someone or just to do something period, do it, and then watch the outcome of your obedience.

Finally, we go out on our first date around the second month of us

Chapter 2: Being Led

knowing each other. Not really having a plan on where it is we wanted to go, we decide to get a cup of coffee and head to a park near the water. I remember getting out of his car and feeling a little breezy as we continue to walk into the park. He asked if I was cold, "Yes," I replied. He then told me that he would give me the shirt off his back to wrap around me to help warm me up. Looking at him with this expression on my face like yeah right, I softly said, "You don't have to do that I'll be alright." He must have known I was lying because he did just what he said he would do. I stood there with a triple extra large peach long sleeved shirt on while he stood there in his white tank top t-shirt. His body reminded me of a football player. Broad shoulders and nice sized chest with a graceful amount of hair that showed above the neck line of his t-

Chapter 2: Being Led

shirt, khaki pants and a pair of brown shoes standing there looking like he was part of a defensive line. "Aren't you cold," I asked? He said, "I will be alright I just didn't want you to be cold." Thanking him, we walk over to this bench and he takes a seat while I stand in front of him. Lamar then tells me he wants me to listen to something. Pulling his cell phone from the case on his waist, he begins to dial this number, which was his voice mail. Lamar played every voice message that I left him back to me. He kept all my messages and replayed them just to hear my voice. Even the messages I sent concerning the purchase of my Pt Cruiser he kept. I'm thinking ok he must really be interested in me. Who does that?

Looking into his eyes, I could tell that he wanted me to be someone more

Chapter 2: Being Led

in his life than a friend. Now this man has given me the shirt off his back and replayed all the messages I left him back to me; he seems cool and he loves Christ he just might be the one. Eventually we lean towards each other and we kiss. Slipping his tongue in my mouth, he pulls me closer to him and wraps his arms around my waist while he gently caresses my back. So gentle, so soft, so passionate, it felt so nice. My heart was screaming what on earth are you doing, but my mind was saying you've been with one man for eleven years and have not been touched since your divorce five years ago. This fills soooo good. After all, he fits the description of the man who I believed is part of my destiny. While all of my alarms were going off, I still embrace the passionate kiss. We stop and look each other in the eye trying to see how the other felt about the kiss.

Chapter 2: Being Led

Instead of saying anything, we hug and begin to walk back to the car. While he's smiling, I'm thinking what in the world have I done. I don't want to play with this man's emotions because my heart was still with Pastor Black. I sit quietly in the front seat of his Chrysler 300 looking out of the window pondering on why did I let this go so far; I begin to repent asking Daddy to forgive me for going this far with someone who may not even be part of my destiny and allowing him in my space.

    Calling him up the next day I told him how I was feeling and how he was the first person since my divorce that I allowed to come into my space. Allowing him in my space means he was able to get pass a surface hug. I tried to convince Lamar that I was placed in his life to encourage him and

Chapter 2: Being Led

to pray for him not get into a relationship with him. Therefore, I began to sow into his life seeds that I believed would help him get even closer to his destiny and purpose in life. The place were I fellowshipped was having a conference for men with Bishop Long so I brought him a ticket for the gathering. I began to sow in his life anything that was spiritually connected to his destiny. Whether it was a compact disc, books, the preached word of God, it didn't matter. I just wanted him to do extremely well in fulfilling his purpose and destiny. I would ask him to pray for me and with me that both of us could develop a richer prayer life. I then begin to see a stem grow out of the soil in which I was able to sow seed.

Lamar was able to see my genuine love for Christ and for him to

Chapter 2: Being Led

prosper in every area of his life, which made him want to be with me even the more. I remember Lamar calling me one day and I could sense in his voice that he wanted to tell me something. Before he could tell me what he wanted to say I told him, I said "You want to love me don't you?" He said, "Yes," but he was afraid because when he tends to love a person he loves them beyond his love for Christ. I told him, "Well don't do that." Therefore, when Lamar started telling me how much he loved me I would respond, "Don't love me more than Christ." I told him that because I didn't want to be an idol in his life. Ladies and gentleman whenever you are in a relationship don't allow that person to love you more than they love Christ. We as people never want to become an idol in someone's life, because if you think about it biblically God destroyed every

Chapter 2: Being Led

idol. If you are a believer in Christ or not, mostly everyone has heard of the commandment which says thou shall have no other god before Me (Exodus 20:3, Deuteronomy 5:7).

Chapter 2: Sow Seed in the Right Season and Soil

Sow Seed In The Right Season And Soil!!!

Time will always tell if you sowed a seed in good soil or not. In the earlier paragraph, I told you that the seed that was sown started to grow into a stem, which made me excited because I thought I was getting ready to see some leaves, some type of plant, or fruit sprout up. After awhile the stem that started to grow starts to wither and dry up. Matthew 13 talks about the person who sows the seed and some fell by the way side, some amongst thorns, some on stony ground, and some produce a thirty, sixty, and hundredfold harvest (Matthew 13: 4-8). When we see destiny from afar off we tend to sow seeds that we believe will produce a harvest, but yet no harvest has manifested or there is a counterfeit harvest one that looks like it's going to

Chapter 2: Sow Seed in the Right Season and Soil

grow but ends up withering away. I saw a stem growing in the soil that I sowed the seed in. For a season, we prayed together; for a season, I saw him change into the man that I believe God was showing me. That means for a moment the harvest looked like it was ripe, but the person who he truly was or how he actually operated came forth.

This is what happens when we sow into destiny that may have never been from God and we operate out of the timing of God. It may produce a harvest, but a crop that will eventually die. A counterfeit harvest!!!!! Wow!!!!!!! A counterfeit harvest may look real and sometimes act real, but eventually truth arises and you realize it wasn't what it looked or acted like at all. Example: You meet a male (females) or female (males) and he or

Chapter 2: Sow Seed in the Right Season and Soil

she is everything you were looking to have in a relationship, they dress nice, have their own home, good line of credit, can hold a mature conversation, etc. Consequently, this type of behavior goes on for about two to three months and you are like 'wow' he or she just might be the one. All of a sudden they get tired of playing the role and you go out and the person you thought was that loving, kind, gentle, meek person who seemed to have all the qualities you are looking for turns out to be just the opposite. That's what we call the counterfeit. How can we avoid the counterfeit? This is a good question. We have to wait on the timing of God and not be in a rush to please our flesh or put a patch over the wound that's in our emotions from previous relationships. What if we don't believe in God then you test yourself by saying is the person I want

Chapter 2: Sow Seed in the Right Season and Soil

to start a relationship with more appeasing to my flesh or is my heart really speaking for me? Don't allow one's emotions to speak, but one's heart.

Chapter 3: Power of Persuasion

Power of Persuasion!!!

I started talking to some of my family members and friends about Lamar and why I believe I was put in his life and how just a little after two months he tells me he loves me. My question to them was how is it possible for someone to start loving you only after two months of knowing you? It didn't make any sense to me. I was a very analytical person back then so I needed stuff to add up. In addition, because Lamar went back to his old ways it was hard for me to believe that he truly loved me.

I told them the whole story about sowing and so forth, and how it only worked for a season now the real Lamar is coming out. I was in a battle with my mind because the characteristics of this man did not line

Chapter 3: Power of Persuasion

up with the characteristics of the man I saw in my dreams. As a result, he couldn't be the person God had ordained as part of my destiny. That's what I would tell myself and then I would listen to my best friend and my sister who reassured me he wasn't the person and to just stick with the vision that I saw. My mom and co-worker response to me was Khadijah you cannot change a man and you need to continue to give the man a chance. They go on to tell me that he might just be the person God is sending you to be your husband, but because you are looking at what you see as his faults you just might miss it. My mom and co-worker overruled my sister and friend. Lamar was tangible; I could touch him I could feel him unlike Pastor Black whom I had no contact with except via e-mail or me going to see him minister every now and then.

Chapter 3: Power of Persuasion

Listening to their advice, I continued to talk to Lamar and we continued to meet for lunch or go and get pedicures followed with massages together. He showed me so much attention and he made me feel as if I was the only person that existed in his world. Sometimes I felt like he would check out the surroundings in the public places before he would show any affection towards me. Even though I felt this way, I brushed it off by saying to myself don't be insecure he is not like your last relationship. In the public eye, he was very, very affectionate. We would always do lunch at least once a week and spend time together when he got off work.

One night when he left work, we decided to meet at the River Walk in downtown Jacksonville. He always told me that I liked the simple things in

Chapter 3: Power of Persuasion

life. Just walking along the waterfront and eating a hot dog was enough for me and that was one of the things that made him love me even more. Lamar told me how he usually dated women that he had to spend money, buy expensive gifts, and pay their bills. Then here I come not asking for anything but to spend time together and that was different for him.

Lamar's favorite question to me would be, "Where did you come from, because I've never met anyone like you." My response to him would be from my mother's womb, but I knew what he was talking about. He was having an experience with someone that was totally opposite from the type of woman he normally dated. I never wanted anything materialistic from Lamar. All I wanted was his time, affection, and communication.

Chapter 3: Power of Persuasion

We meet at the River Walk one night and we stroll down the trail holding hands and looking at the stillness of the water it was nice and peaceful. Lamar and I joke around a little bit then eventually find a place to sit down. This time I sit while he stands in front of me. As he stands there, he tells me how beautiful I am and how he has never met a woman like me before. I tell him how I have never met a man like him before who showed me so much attention. I could tell he had fallen for me and I was really starting to dig him also. Again, we kiss and embrace one another with so much passion how long and how sweet then all of a sudden, he pushes me back and states how he could not take it anymore. I'm looking at him like what!!!!!!!! I asked him what's wrong and he just said, "I can't take it anymore let's go."

Chapter 3: Power of Persuasion

I get in my car and before he gets in his car, he asked me to follow him. He takes me down these side streets and makes all these different turns when he finally slows down right when we get by these bright lights on the front of this building. As we pull up closer I look up towards the lights and the name on the building was the Hyatt. Parking our cars, we go inside and he pays for a room. I'm chuckling inside saying to myself what on earth I hope he doesn't think he is getting any of my cookies. We take the elevator up to the room and Lamar unlocks the door.

We walk inside, I put my purse on the table, and he walks on the right side of the bed taking off his shoes and lies down. Standing by the left side of the bed in my mind, I am saying this joker must be crazy to think that he is

Chapter 3: Power of Persuasion

going to get a bite of my cookies. He invites me to lie down beside him assuring me that he doesn't want to have sex with me he just wants to cuddle. I sit down on the edge of the bed, kick off my shoes, and lie down next to him. He turns on the television and we began to watch whatever was on. Eventually he leans over and kisses me and I kiss him back assuring him that he wasn't getting any of my cookies and how I just wanted to rest. He put his arm around me; I laid my head on his chest, and we continued watching television until I fell asleep. Feeling him get up he told me he had to leave because he had to get up early the next morning for work and for me to get some rest. After he leaves, I leave to and get me some clothes for the next day. I come back, take a shower, jump in my comfy hotel bed and sleep like a baby.

Chapter 3: Power of Persuasion

The next morning after checking out, I head to Lamar's job. We sit and talk for a few minutes going over what happened that night before. He tells me that was his first time paying for a hundred dollar hotel room that he didn't get to use. A week or so later we go out to eat at Outback Steakhouse and while we were waiting to be served, I reached in my purse and pull out this box that contained a pair of my panties sprayed with perfume and told Lamar this is the closest you are going to get to my cookies. I did that as a joke thinking he was going to give them back to me but he kept them.

It's going on three months since Lamar and I have been dating each other. Lamar used to always call me night or day and tell me he needed to

Chapter 3: Power of Persuasion

see me or sometimes I would call him and let him know that I am going to stop by his job for a hug or a kiss or just to be in each other's company. So therefore, I would go to him or we would meet some place and after he sees me he would say that he was much better. I didn't know a hug could be so powerful, until Lamar told me years later. Dag I was green.

    This particular night when he called I knew something was different and even though my heart was telling me not to go, I did it anyway. We meet at this a golf course parking lot and I park next to him while he sat in his black Lincoln Navigator. I get out of my car as he gets out the driver's side, and we hug each other and chat for a little bit then we both get in the back seat of the Navigator. We start to embrace each other with hugs and

Chapter 3: Power of Persuasion

kisses to the point that I began to give into the heat of the moment. Lamar slowly pulls my tucked shirt from out of my pants, moves his hand gently upward towards my breast, and caresses them ever so softly. I became heated and I straddled my body across his and began to kiss him on his neck down to his chest as I unbuttoned his shirt. Lamar then unbuckles his belt and then starts to unbutton his pants at this point I didn't have a care in the world because even though he did this I felt we could just engage in the foreplay without having the sex. Even though he unbuttoned his pants and pulled them down to his ankles, I wasn't worried about becoming intimate because mine were still on. Until he said baby your pants are rough so guess what he unbuttons them and down slides my pants too. There we were in our shirts and

Chapter 3: Power of Persuasion

underwear me straddling him while we continue to kiss on each other, my tongue in his ear and lips wrapped around my breast we were going at it. Lamar then said baby you are so wet and feel so good I just want to be in you. I told him, "No, I'm not going that far it's not of God. That's fornicating."

    Pause: look at me talking about God during foreplay. His response was baby the Lord will forgive you. Keep in mind we are having a conversation between each kiss, tongue in the ear, etc. Things got quiet and I noticed that he started pulling my panties to one side slipping his penis into my vagina we begin having sex. Now all kinds of thoughts were running through my mind at the time, but I overrode all of them with my flesh. I didn't bother to stop him even

Chapter 3: Power of Persuasion

though I was battling in my mind between this feeling so good and oh my goodness what am I doing? We continue with our intimate moment and Lamar starts asking me to promise him I will never leave him, and so I felt he was asking something of me that I could not promise him.

    I wasn't exactly sure who he was in my life. I didn't know if he was part of my destiny or not. Most of the time it's women who want the men to stay in their lives forever after they have been intimate, but to have a man ask a woman to promise to never leave him was new to me. I didn't know what to say or do. We end our intimate moment by embracing each other with a hug and me laying my head on his shoulder and saying I just went against the will of the Father and fornicated. Lamar looked at me and said, "Are

Chapter 3: Power of Persuasion

you crying?" I told him, "No," but I did feel conviction settle in.

The reason I put so much detail is because I wanted to show how easy it is to fall into sin or step out of the will of God if only for that moment. We were two people caught up in the lust of our flesh and at that time, we didn't care about condoms or diseases. I thought I was strong enough to handle the passion of a kiss or control the lust of my flesh, but I found out that I really wasn't.

After it was all over and we departed from each other, I started thinking about how I judged this woman for committing adultery on her husband. I had no compassion in my heart for her at all. I would say to myself and a friend of mine how can she say she loves God, go out, and

Chapter 3: Power of Persuasion

commit adultery. She broke the covenant between her and her husband and her and God about her act of sin. I had so much to say. Now here I am so many years later in 2007 doing the same thing. Even though he wasn't married and I wasn't married I still did the same thing.

Matthew chapter seven talks about judging people and when you judge someone you will be judged with the same measure you judged that person (paraphrased- Matthew 7:1-2). I fell into the same sin and found myself repenting and asking God to forgive me for judging her and for stepping out of His will. So much was going through my mind I started thinking okay he got what he wanted; there is no way he would want to continue in this relationship even though he asked me to never leave him. I felt he was

Chapter 3: Power of Persuasion

saying that because of the moment of us being intimate. I would always say that if a person persuades you to go against the will of God for your life or step out of His will, then that person is not the person for you. That is how I felt about Lamar that he could not have been the person God wants me to marry because I've already stepped out of the will of the Father.

We didn't talk to each other until the next day about two or three o'clock that afternoon. Everything that I thought that he would do or how he would respond he didn't. He did totally the opposite. He starts telling me how he doesn't ever want me to leave him and how much he loves me and so on. I remember going to meet him for lunch one Wednesday and when we finished lunch, Lamar starts to pray over me to be his wife. I

Chapter 3: Power of Persuasion

laughed because that was so funny to me. Even though he did pray, my mind was still wrapped around this couldn't be true because how could he allow me to step outside of the will of God. Yeah I pushed the blame and started to divert my attention back to the dream I had and the person who was in the dream, Pastor Black.

Chapter 4: Back to the Dream

Back to the Dream!!!

When I would e-mail Pastor Black, I would occasionally put my cell phone number at the bottom of the e-mail hoping that one day he would call. I sent him a particular e-mail that the Holy Spirit downloaded to me which featured some of his past, present and future. To my surprise, he called me. I remember standing in my kitchen checking my voice mails and I hear his voice saying, "Khadijah this is Pastor Black. I got your e-mail; give me a call." He left his number. While listening to the voice message, I started breaking out in sweat bubbles feeling as if butterflies were flying all around in my stomach. I was so nervous I didn't know what to do. Should I call him immediately or should I wait? I paced back and forth in front of the kitchen sink listening to that voice

Chapter 4: Back to the Dream

mail over and over until I made the decision to call him. I was so nervous I didn't know what he was going to say or how I would respond to what he would say.

This could be the beginning of my destiny being fulfilled. His phone rings at least three to four times before he answers. He said, "Khadijah I was on the other line, but I did want to make sure I get a chance to talk to you." He tells me, "Thank you for sending me that e-mail." He asked me something that made me respond by saying, "I'm trying to keep from entertaining the counterfeits." We talked a little more and before we hung up, he tells me to make sure I read the next day's message and I told him that I always do.

Chapter 4: Back to the Dream

The next day comes and I can't wait to get home from work so I can read the message that he had sent out. Sitting at my sister's computer reading this message that talks about Eve the wife of Adam, had me blown away. I started wondering was he directing this to me. Saying to myself, he had to be because he would have never told me to make sure I read it. The e-mail went something like this, '...These letters are to speak to you from afar as you begin the final portion of your journey that will bring you to me and me to you. As Adam, all of the sons of God wait in expectation of the arrival of she who must come. Eve, you are not optional and I Adam cannot and will not finish my purpose without you. So, I send this letter to you in full hope that as you read this and I know you will. That through this letter you will understand why I took so long and

Chapter 4: Back to the Dream

why you had to go through the pain of entertaining the counterfeits for so long before the arrival of the promise and cutting of the covenant (paraphrased)...' After I read this message, I was sure that he knew who I was to be in his life and I definitely felt like I knew he was part of my destiny. Mr. and Mrs. Black what a name. I started cheesing from ear to ear. The hope that once died now was resurrected. Pastor Black knows I am his wife; God must have shown him were the thoughts going through my head.

I started going to support him even the more whenever he was close to Jacksonville, Florida. It didn't matter what time he was to speak I would go and then turn around and drive back home. I felt like Ruth gleaning from Boaz's field. Ruth had

Chapter 4: Back to the Dream

to be discovered by Boaz in order for her to get her full blessing. When I would go and support him, it was so weird.

One time my kids and I went to a youth conference where he was the guest speaker for the night. At a point in the time of him ministering, he asked all the young men to come to the altar and so my sons went up to the altar for prayer. After it was over and they began to release the congregation, my boys went back up to speak to Pastor Black. A few minutes later they run back to me and say, "Mommy Pastor Black wants to see you." So I go and he speaks and says, "Stick around. Some of us are going out to eat." He wanted us to join him. Hours went by and we are still waiting. Finally, we leave and head to the restaurant and the waiter sits us at a

Chapter 4: Back to the Dream

different table away from those who came with him.

Meanwhile, the kids and I were at a table by ourselves. Eventually Pastor Black comes to his table and sits down to eat and they were just enjoying their fellowship and ignoring us as if we didn't exist. I don't know if he forgot he invited us, got distracted, or just was out right ignoring us, but I know I was fed up. I am saying to the kids how is it he invites us out to eat and then just ignores us as if we don't exist. We eat our meal and I pay for it, got my receipt and tell them bye. Pastor Black stops us as if he really forgot that we were there. He talks to us for a moment and then walks us to the door, prays for us and tells us he loves us. When he said that I thought he was talking to the kids so I didn't respond.

Chapter 4: Back to the Dream

Then he stops me before I can get out of the door and tells me, "I love you." I said, "I love you too." He tells me to call him at the hotel when we are settled.

This is how it has been for the past few years. It's has always been an ignore I see you kind of thing. I see you when I want your attention, but I am going to ignore you when I think you want my attention. It's truly been a roller coaster that I allowed to take place in my emotions. Thinking he loves me, he loves me not, he loves me, he loves me not. I thank God for healing me because I can look as this and laugh at me. Back to the story…

Even though my heart was with Pastor Black the man of God in my dreams, my flesh was craving Lamar the man I had been intimate with. I

Chapter 4: Back to the Dream

had a desire to be with him sexually until I didn't care where or when. My desire was to fulfill the lust of my flesh. I never knew what an addict felt like until I had this experience with Lamar. I craved to be with him just as much as he wanted to be with me. I would call him just to meet him so that we could have that sexual experience and sometimes he would call me and we would meet and go at it. Hampton Inn, Hyatt, Navigator, wherever, it didn't matter because we wanted to get our fix.

    I am telling you sex can be addictive. I never had an experience with drugs thank God, but I have heard that when you go through a withdrawal from drugs your body starts going through changes. For example, a person may start twitching, having bad headaches, skin discoloration, or loose

Chapter 4: Back to the Dream

weight. Well with sex, your body goes through different changes too. When you have sex, your breasts get bigger along with your hips. (Mothers and fathers this is one sign that you can look for when you think your child is sexual) When you are going through withdrawals one experiences the vagina throbbing, stomach warbling, and restlessness. You try to cross your legs to stop your vagina from throbbing or take a shower hoping that this will all go away. These were some of my experiences.

However, as time goes on it seems like sometimes when the craving would come upon me and I wanted to make arrangements to meet nothing would happen. At night when I would go through withdrawals, I had to get up, take a cold shower, speak to me, and tell me not tonight. I prayed

Chapter 4: Back to the Dream

that the Lord would take the desire that I had for Lamar out of my flesh. It did not happen overnight; it was a process. I had to continue not to give into the lust of my flesh no matter how many times my vagina started throbbing or flashbacks of us caressing each other and how good it would feel at that moment. Khadijah had to do the work in denying her flesh and pulling down the strongholds that were in her mind.

At the time when I was intimate with Lamar, I was willing to override everything that the Holy Ghost was telling me and showing me. The Lord would show me in dreams that I would be exposed if I didn't stop what I was doing. Nobody knew that I was intimate with Lamar. I was still working in ministry and still praying for people still functioning, but not in

Chapter 4: Back to the Dream

full capacity. I was torn between the two, because one of them I had no real connection with besides e-mail and when I would go and support him.

Even when I would go and support Pastor Black, sometimes he would acknowledge and talk with me and sometimes he would just ignore me as if I wasn't even there. Then I had a man who was right here in my face calling me everyday telling me he loves me, how beautiful I am, and giving me all the attention I would ever need from a male. Lamar also had some of the same qualities as Pastor Black.

As time progressed from 2007 into the last part of 2008, I ended up giving the majority of my time and effort to Lamar. We were intimate at least eight other times and during the

Chapter 4: Back to the Dream

course of our relationship, I never knew where he stayed and I never got to meet his mom or other family members. We didn't spend any holidays together and this led me to believe that he was truly hiding something.

Besides, the Lord kept His promise to me and exposed me. I remember one day I was at work and one of my co-workers saw a hickey, passion mark on my neck. She yelled out, "What are you doing with a passion mark on your neck? You are supposed to be a Christian setting a good example." I was so ashamed and embarrassed all I could say is that a righteous man may fall down seven times and gets back up (Proverbs 24:16). I told her my goal is to get back up.

Chapter 4: Back to the Dream

From that point, I really had to do self-examination of what my real purpose was for staying in a relationship with Lamar. Driving down 95 North I was talking to the Lord and He showed me that I was just using him for my sexual pleasure, because in my heart I knew that he was not the man God had ordained for me. For that reason, I called him and told him that I was very sorry for using him for my pleasure. Lamar accepted my apology, but in turn allowed me to know that he was using me for his pleasure too. Needless to say, our relationship ended around the end of 2008. Even though we kept in touch with each other, we haven't been intimate since that time. Now that it's 2010 going into 2011, our communication with one another is scarce. When we do talk it's like a blast from the past with him not able to

Chapter 4: Back to the Dream

move beyond what we had intimately. This leaves me praying that the Lord will heal his soul.

I asked Lamar to write something for this book and this is what he wrote, "When two people are in a relationship one must know his or her boundaries. Because when you meet, everyone has a different motive. Some people are out to see what they can get. Some are just out to have sex and some are really sincere. As you engage in a relationship, please make sure that everyone is on the same page. A person can come into a relationship with one motive and end up falling in love. So always, define your purpose in one's life. Always remember this because you can still be in love with someone and they have moved on." Wow enough said. I still support Pastor Black mainly through prayer. I

Chapter 4: Back to the Dream

haven't e-mailed him since the beginning of this year being 2010 and the last time I went to support him or celebrate with him was at his birthday party in 2009 when he turned thirty-six. Pastor Black is now happily married.

At times, it was hard to move on especially when you believe God has shown you destiny. Even though the Lord showed me at least three times in a dream that Pastor Black would get married and it wouldn't be to me. I still wanted to try to hold onto the one dream I had years before. Even before Pastor Black got married, a close friend would always tell me that if he were to marry and divorce I am still Mrs. Black. We were decreeing that I am Mrs. Black silly stuff, stupid stuff. (Pastor Black if you ever get to read this I speak longevity to your

Chapter 4: Back to the Dream

marriage!) It's funny now, but at the time we really believed what we were saying. I believe that the Lord allowed me to go through these things to release this book into the lives of others that may have seen what or whom they believe destiny was and pursued it ahead of time immaturely, or didn't receive the full revelation of what God was saying to them.

Chapter 5: The Revelation

The Revelation!!!

I've realized that when we pursue after destiny prematurely we end up giving birth in the twenty-six week term instead of the thirty-six week period. Sometimes pain, rejection, hurt, anger, or bitterness will make us try to fulfill destiny at its early stages. Because we don't want to go through the process of being healed or we think that if we pursue after what we believe is part of our destiny the hurt, pain rejection and bitterness will go away. Without inner healing, these things can influence you to reject the real timing of God that would connect us with our destiny. While writing this book, I had the awesome privilege of taking a healing class given by my apostolic leader at that time Dr. Clark that brought so

Chapter 5: The Revelation

much revelation and clarity towards my reason for pursuing destiny.

I had a steady male in my life from 1991 until the mid 2002; when my ex-husband and I separated then divorced in October of 2005, it left me with open wounds. Then having this dream, several months later about this anointed man of God proposing to me didn't help me any, it made me cuckoo. I was up and down, I believed and then I didn't. Through the hurt, I have experienced which came from rejection, lack of feeling loved and verbal abuse that leads to low self-esteem, I started to pursue after destiny trying to fill those voided places in my life. All it did was add more hurt, pain, rejection and low-self esteem on top of what was already there. Instead of taking the time to be healed, I tried to be fulfilled.

Chapter 5: The Revelation

When we fill a container that still has holes in it, eventually it empties out. Instead of fixing the holes we will go back and try to fill it again with the same stuff, maybe we will use a substance that is stronger, or thicker that won't easily flow through the holes. The point is that it's still going to leak because we never fixed the holes. Another analogy is we can use is when we fill a weakened container with goods, it's going to burst because it's too weak to hold the goods. Instead of us getting a stronger container, we try to patch up the old container and fill it back up when we know it's not strong enough to hold those goods. If you look at the two analogies that I gave you notice that one container had holes while the other container was weak. The holes represent a voided place in a person's life. The weakened container is not one

Chapter 5: The Revelation

with holes, but it is one with no strength. It is the container that allows a person to be defeated by the same cycles in life without ever finding the strength to become victorious. This is what happened in my life with these two gentlemen.

Rather than taking the time to be completely healed, I became my own physician and prescribed my own medication, which did not heal any of my wounds, but brought a greater infection. I once took one dose of hurt, pain, and rejection a day which created a small wound from past relationships. Nevertheless, when I started on this emotional roller coaster I went from one dose to two extra doses that created an extremely large wound. How did I let myself get this wounded, which brought on an infirmity of unbelief, and a lack of

Chapter 5: The Revelation

trust towards God and man? The Holy Spirit showed me that I didn't allow myself to get healed; I didn't know my identity, and I didn't wait on the timing of the Lord.

Having that dream about Pastor Black gave me some type of hope of someone loving me again, confidence was coming back to me and my self-esteem was rising. Furthermore, at one point he was showing me the attention that I needed. Then after the e-mail rejection settled in on top of what was already there, taking a class helped me to identify the symptoms of rejection and get to the root to where it all began.

My first experience with rejection started when I was young and because I didn't recognize it I never got healed; so it stayed with me

Chapter 5: The Revelation

through adulthood. I had to first revisit that place in my childhood and ask the Lord to bring healing to that area from way back then. I had to forgive and learn how to be ok with being rejected. I also learned how not to let rejection keep me bound in fear. That means don't give up on your dreams. Don't be afraid to ask or get things started because of the fear of being turned down or turned away. I haven't given up because of what I have experienced in past relationships, because I know that God still has a plan for me and my babies.

The definition of rejection is as follows: not wanted, unsatisfactory, or not fulfilling the standard requirement. Here are some nuggets that will help you to realize if you are experiencing rejection.

Chapter 5: The Revelation

- Rejection will keep you isolated.
- Rejection will altar your decision-making.
- Rejection will make you loose the confidence you have in you.
- Rejection will make you doubt God.
- Rejection can make you move out of the timing and season without ever being healed.
- Rejection will make you look for love in all the wrong places. Instead of seeking Him who is Love, Jesus Christ. If you find any of these things going on in your life, you might want to find out when you first experienced rejection.

Chapter 5: Feeling Unworthy or of Little to No Value

Feeling Unworthy or of Little to No Value!!!

The definition of value is to think that something is important and meaningful: what something is worth. Life's ups and downs can rob us from truly identifying with the value that dwells on the inside of us. For example my siblings used to call me banana because I was lighter than them in color. So I desired for my skin color to change to a darker color to fit in with them. I didn't accept the color that God created me to be because I didn't know my self worth. This mindset followed me through my school years all the way to adulthood. During my school years things that I wouldn't normally do, I did to fit in with the crowd. I became passive to many things.

Chapter 5: Feeling Unworthy or of Little to No Value

When I was in the tenth or eleventh grade, I dated a guy that started to cheat on me with another girl and treat me like crap. Because I didn't value myself, I stayed in that relationship for years until I got fed up and said enough is enough. Then years later I entered into another relationship with that same passive mentality and instead of saying enough is enough we married. I never healed; I never looked at me and said you are valuable; you are worth more than how you are being treated. After my divorce, I entered another relationship that was similar to the first two. I never caught him cheating but I just felt something was wrong in our relationship. However, because of the attention, and a need to feel loved I tried to look pass the obvious.

Chapter 5: Feeling Unworthy or of Little to No Value

I remember one day I was at my mom's house the doorbell rang and it was this woman that wanted to know about my relationship with Lamar. All the things Lamar was telling me, he also was telling her. Now most women would have clicked, but I didn't. I stayed calm and listened to her story. After she got finished, I prayed for her and she went on her way.

Did Lamar and I break up? No because I still didn't know my worth. I didn't fully understand that I was created in the image and likeness of God and He gave me beauty for ashes. I didn't realize that I have this treasure that dwells on the inside of me. It took some time and self examination after our break up for me to realize that it wasn't Lamar who treated me as if I had no value, it was I who allowed me

Chapter 5: Feeling Unworthy or of Little to No Value

to be treated this way. We are so quick to blame others for our downfalls instead of examining ourselves to find that weak area that's in our souls; this is what causes us to accept this type of treatment.

Chapter 5: The Soul of a Man

The Soul of a Man!!!

Let's talk about what dwells in the soul of a man. The soul consists of your will, emotions, mind, intellect and imagination. The weakest area in my life was my emotions. Emotion is defined as a state of mind in which feeling, sentiment, or attitude is predominant (over cognition and volition). Our emotions have the ability to override our conscious awareness even our own will.

This is what happened to me. The past wounds of rejection, low self-esteem, intimidation, insecurity and what I thought was the need to feel loved by someone, led me to become a slave to what I call emotional manipulation. Emotional manipulation is anything that makes you respond to the open wound that's in your heart

Chapter 5: The Soul of a Man

that has never been healed. For example, you go through a divorce or break-up and then you hear a song on the radio or you watch a movie about love. Then you respond to that manipulation by calling up an old friend knowing all the while that you are not interested in him or her if you are a female or male on the rebound. Emotional manipulation comes in so many different shapes and forms.

In the pages of this book, you now can plainly see the places I gave into emotional manipulation. There were times I knew what I was doing was wrong but because my flesh longed for attention, I gave in to the manipulation of man. He was just doing his job. It was up to me to think more of myself to put a stop the deceitfulness of my emotions.

Chapter 5: The Soul of a Man

Emotions can be such a deception to you and to those who are among you. I knew from the start that I wasn't going to build a long lasting relationship with Lamar, but because of the need to fill those wounded places in my heart I deceived him through my emotions. Instead of pulling back and saying Lamar I know this isn't going to work I allowed him to fall in love until he said enough is enough. Then vice versa, I knew some of the things Lamar said and did were a lie that he was not healed in some areas in his life because of past hurts. So he manipulated me through his emotions and guess what I let him. It is so vitally important that before we enter into another relationship or make any big decision that we make sure that our open wounds are healed. That we start to view ourselves as God does.

Chapter 5: God's View of Us

God's View of Us!!!!

First of all, according to the word of God we were created in his image and his likeness. *Then God said, "Let us make man in Our image, according to Our likeness, and let them rule over the fish of the sea and over the birds of the sky and over the cattle over all the earth, and over every creeping thing that creeps the earth. 27 And God created man in His own image; in the image of God He created him; male and female (Genesis 1: 26-27 NASB).*

In the beginning we were made (to bring into being, form) in God's image; therefore holiness was already in us, godliness was already in us, a purity of heart was already in us, joy was already in us, love was already in us, and worship, power, and authority was already in us. Then He gave us a

Chapter 5: God's View of Us

function He said, "Let them rule over the fish of the sea and over the birds of the sky and over the cattle and over all the earth and over every creeping thing that creeps on the earth." All of these characteristics were given to us from the foundation of the world.

Chapter 6: My Life's Journey

My Life's Journey!!!

When I was born into the world I was the cutest and precious little baby there was at least that is what I was told. By the time I was three or four my mom told me that I was very bold and I was a fighter. She said when the boys would mess with my brother; I would go to where he was and bite them on the leg. My mom said that after they knocked me down I would get up and come home put some petroleum jelly on my bruises and go back to fighting.

Between the ages of five and six years old, we left Philadelphia and moved to North Carolina and I a got a chance to meet five of my older siblings that I never knew. Being the youngest of what was once one sibling to now being the youngest of six

Chapter 6: My Life's Journey

siblings I wanted to fit in. Yet, it wasn't that simple; we are all meeting each other for the first time. So, the best I could have gotten out of them was toleration. Truly embracing me as their younger sister probably didn't come till some months or years later. This was my first experience with rejection.

When I was in middle school, I was teased a lot because I had a big forehead. Therefore, different ones started calling me 'go head forehead.' These words pierced me and I covered up my forehead with my hair. I didn't stop covering up my forehead until the end of my high school year. Low self-esteem was created in me from those words.

By the time I entered into my tenth grade year in high school I was

Chapter 6: My Life's Journey

already harboring low self-esteem and rejection. My goal in high school was to find a group of people that I couldn't fit in with or those I thought were better than me thinking this will help build my self-esteem. Have you ever heard the saying don't hang around people just like you, but those that are going somewhere. This can be good and bad. It can be good if you learn from their example, but for me I didn't learn good things. I became insecure and started doing things out of my character trying to be better than them. Now I have insecurity, low self-esteem, rejection and a whole bunch of other stuff that I just didn't name residing on the inside of me. We are talking about my life's journey and how words and the actions of people have the ability to become one's identity.

Chapter 6: My Life's Journey

I accepted Jesus Christ as my Lord and Savior at the age of eighteen and the baptism of the Holy Spirit came in my late twenties. These behaviors didn't leave but they were still there and followed me into my marriage. I've realized that getting a divorce was not all my ex-husband's fault; I had a role to play in it too. Even still after my divorce, I added bitterness and the ability to not forgive those whom I felt have wounded me. Again, these characteristics dwelt within me during my emotional roller coaster with Lamar and Pastor Black.

Being a Christian (Christ like), I was taught that things get better once you get saved. Well when the things that I thought were supposed to get better got worst, I started to doubt God. Then I was told I needed deliverance, so I went to a deliverance

Chapter 6: My Life's Journey

service. Months later characteristics of unbelief, rejection, bitterness, low self-esteem would manifest right back in my life. I am not saying that deliverance services don't work nor am I saying that when you become a son of God things won't get better, all I am saying is that there is more to it than what I was taught.

Chapter 6: What Does It Mean To Be Christ Like

What Does It Mean To Be Christ Like?

Based on man's perspective and some of the biblical scriptures they've added to their perspective. They have made Christ like to be a law saying Christians don't do this and Christians don't do that. Christians don't listen to secular music; they are to forgive those that have harmed them. Even though I followed these principles but still somehow, those ways and tendencies would come back. I am a Christian going to service every time the doors open, taking notes, come home studying what was taught but still not delivered.

Let's take a look at the scripture*: Romans 8: 11-14 NASB*
11. But if the Spirit of Him who raised Jesus from the dead dwells in

Chapter 6: What Does It Mean To Be Christ Like

you, He who raised Christ Jesus from the dead will also give life to your mortal bodies through His Spirit who indwells you. 12. So then, brethren, we are under obligation, not to the flesh, to live according to the flesh 13. for if you are living according to the flesh you must die; but if by the Spirit you are putting to death the deeds of the body, you will live. 14. For all who are being led by the Spirit of God these are sons of God.

From the beginning, God created us in His image and likeness that means He created us as spirit beings first. Romans 8:11 states, *that if the Spirit of Him who raised Jesus from the dead dwells in you...* This scripture blessed me so much because it made me realize that I needed the indwelling of His Spirit and the function of His Spirit is to give life to my mortal body.

Chapter 6: What Does It Mean To Be Christ Like

When God was speaking to creation, He thought about us and made us like Himself. That means everything we need to overcome those ungodly characteristics is already in us.

The characteristics of God are already in us godliness, holiness, love, joy, forgiveness and so much more are already in us. The scripture tells us that when the Holy Spirit dwells on the inside of us that I am no longer obligated to the flesh (paraphrased). I am no longer obligated to respond to life through rejection, doubt, bitterness, and insecurity, but I now can respond to life through love, joy, purity of heart, and godliness. Why? Because the Spirit of God dwells on the inside of me!!!!!! Hallelujah!!! Jesus I am grateful. I had to become one with who God created me to be in the beginning and that's a spirit being.

Chapter 6: What Does It Mean To Be Christ Like

Oh my gosh! I had to go back to the beginning when I was first created before I entered my mother's womb and become one with the Spirit of God as He created me to be. I got tired of going in circles. I had to pray and ask God who am I and how am I supposed to carry myself **beyond** my situations, circumstances, and what and who people say I am?

Chapter 6: Who I Am

Who I Am?

Galatians 4:4-7 NASB 4. But when the fulness of time came, God sent forth His Son, born of a woman, born under the Law, 5. in order that He might redeem those who were under the Law, that we might receive the adoption as sons. 6. And because you are sons, God has sent the Spirit of His Son into our hearts, crying "Abba! Father!" 7. Therefore you are no longer a slave, but a son; and if a son, then an heir through God.

It is because of Jesus Christ that I am able to become a son of God because He has redeemed me. Through salvation, we are redeemed and through His Spirit we become sons. Romans 8:14 states, *For all who are led by the Spirit of God, these are the sons of God.*

Chapter 6: Who I Am

Let's talk about His Spirit who is the Holy Spirit and the Spirit's function. The Holy Spirit has many functions in one's life. He is our Comforter and Teacher Who brings conviction, guidance, and leads us into all truth. When we become one with the Holy Spirit, the characteristics listed above are part of us. That means when we are lonely instead of calling Jon Doe or Susie Q; we go to the Holy Spirit, the Comforter inside of us. We have to access Him on the inside of us given by God Himself and not given by man.

Growing up children had a habit of saying all the time that sticks and stones may break my bones, but words would never hurt me. The later part of this statement for my life I can say is not true. Man's words do hurt, but God gave us the ability to counteract

Chapter 6: Who I Am

those words by His Spirit and through knowing your identity. For me knowing my identity as a son brought me into a belief and trust like never before. I believe my Daddy; I believe His word. I believe His Spirit will lead and guide me into all truth. You can't tell me that the Word of God isn't true. That's just like a child who has close relationship with their natural father; you can't tell that child anything negative about his or her dad. That child believes every word that his or her father says. Well this is how I feel now that I know my identity.

Now that I know my identity and I have a relationship with the Holy Spirit, I am not eager to pursue after destiny without first seeking the leading of the Holy Spirit who leads us into all truth. I am not so quick to entertain every counterfeit that comes

Chapter 6: Who I Am

in front of me because I am comforted. I no longer respond through rejection, hurt, pain, insecurity, bitterness, and low self-esteem, because I am one with the Word of God that says blessed are the pure in heart for they shall see God (Matthew 5:8). I am fearfully and wonderfully made, that He has given me beauty for ashes (Psalms 139:14, Isaiah 61:3). I am not moved by everything anymore and I don't take the negative words or actions to heart anymore. The same way I came into my identity which has carried me into a mindset and heart of believing the Word of God and trusting the Spirit of God like never before is available to whoever is reading this book.

- First step is acknowledging you have a problem.
- Second step is asking God to forgive you all deeds and flesh of

the heart (i.e. sins, iniquities, and transgressions).
- Third, allow Jesus Christ to become Lord over/in your life.
- Fourth, ask for the baptism of with the Holy Spirit with evidence of speaking in tongues.
- Fifth, become one with your new identity as a new creature in Christ Jesus.

Chapter 6: Let's Pray

Let's Pray!!!

Father in the name of Jesus I thank you for allowing me to share my heart with these Your people. I pray that the words on the pages of this book enlighten them, bring clarity and revelation to every situation, and circumstance in their life. Father I pray that as they ask that You will fill them with the Holy Spirit in the name of Jesus. I thank You for the Spirit of truth that is leading and guiding Your people even as they read these passages. I pray that this book will help them to develop a more intimate relationship with You, recognizing that you are truly Abba, Father. Daddy I pray that even as they become one with You that embracing their identity as sons will be easy. Daddy I pray that You are pleased with this book and as a result the people who have read or

Chapter 6: Let's Pray

those who come in contact with someone who has read this book will be transformed even the more into Your image and Your likeness. Father I thank You, honor You and bless You in Jesus name I pray. Amen.

Chapter 6: Let's Pray

References

Philip D. Morehead, Albert Morehead & Loy Morehead. *The New American Webster Handy College Dictionary, 3rd Edition*, 1995. Published by New American Library, New York, NY.

The Open Bible Expanded Edition: New American Standard Bible, Published by World Publishing, 1985.

Order Information
www.eternalimpartation.org
Click link to the Impartation Store

www.amazon.com

www.ingramcontent.com/pod-product-compliance
Lightning Source LLC
Chambersburg PA
CBHW071130090426
42736CB00012B/2081